A GUIDE TO THE LIBRARIES OF

The New York Public Library

The New York Public Library is a nonprofit, tax-exempt
corporation chartered for free public service. The Library
is sustained by a combination of public and private
funds. Private contributions are needed to help provide
the services you want. Please become a FRIEND . . .
ask any librarian or guard for a FRIENDS brochure.

BEYOND THE LIONS A GUIDE TO THE LIBRARIES OF

The New York Public Library

Contents

Acknowledgment
The publication of this Guide has been made possible by a generous grant from
The New York Community Trust.

Prepared by the staff of The New York Public Library.
Introduction and General Description of The New York Public Library by John Heller.
General Editor: John Heller
Designed by Page, Arbitrio & Resen, Ltd.
Printed by Sanders Printing Corp.

Library of Congress Catalog Card Number — 73-87775
International Standard Book Card Number — 0-87104-302-5

Letter from the President

To our users and friends:

The New York Public Library is a vast and complicated network of information sources which stands as one of the world's largest and finest systems. We at the Library feel the public at times is sufficiently confused by this complexity that it fails to take advantage of the many rich services the Library provides.

This guide has been developed in order that all persons — the general reader, researchers, faculty members, businessmen and students — can find the proper level of service. This service ranges from the smallest neighborhood branch, to the larger Borough Library Center, to the specialized collections, to Mid-Manhattan with its combination of research and circulating facilities, and finally to the in-depth resources of The Research Libraries. We hope this Guide will encourage more and better usage of the Library system.

Publication of this book would not have been possible without the generous support of The New York Community Trust, whose concern for the citizens of New York City resulted in a grant to The New York Public Library.
This first edition of the Guide will eventually be out-of-date. We hope, however, that it will be accurate for at least a two-year period; revisions will be made when practical and necessary. The funds received from sale of this edition will be applied to the costs of future ones.
Good browsing, good reading, good research.

R W Couper

Richard W. Couper
President and Chief Executive Officer

Introduction

There is a play by John Guare in which a librarian is eaten by one of the lions that guards the entrance to the Public Library's Central Building on Fifth Avenue. Unfortunately, this delightful bit of theatrical fantasy reflects all too accurately what large numbers of people imagine will happen to them if they should ever set foot inside the Library. Or if not quite ready to believe that they will be swallowed by the lions—or the librarians, for that matter, they are at least braced to be intimidated, bewildered, lost, and confused.

Perhaps this is because in the minds of so many of us The New York Public Library is the Central Building—that vast, monumental structure in whose presence egos quaver and the question arises, "How will I ever find anything in there!" Perhaps there are other reasons. Yet the fact remains that beyond the small and intimate neighborhood branches, well known to those who live nearby, there indeed is trepidation in the face of the Library, and that the air of unfamiliarity that surrounds it prevents numbers of us from using it effectively, or from using it at all.

It is our purpose here to dispel the mysteries and make the Library and its treasures, programs, and services familiar and accessible to everyone.

How to use this Guide

This guide is designed to give you a broad overview of The New York Public Library and to be of practical assistance in using the Library's facilities.

Start with the general description section on page 8 in order to learn how the Library is organized and where you, with your individual requirements as a user, fit into the picture.

The main body of the Guide consists of alphabetically arranged entries describing the Library's collections, installations, research tools, programs, and services.

The Subject Directory, beginning on page 87, is an alphabetical listing which gives the locations of the Library's most extensive collections in each subject. The directory can save you a good deal of time and confusion by leading you straight to your subject. Page numbers shown in the directory refer to entries in this Guide which describe the collections, divisions, departments, and sections of the Library in which the subject is located.

A directory listing the names, addresses, and telephone numbers of all Library buildings starts on page 94.

A removable map showing the locations of all Library buildings is inserted in the book.

Important Reminder: A guide, however complete, can do no more than point out, describe, locate, and instruct. It cannot **use** the Library for you. In the end, you must do this for yourself. But where this Guide leaves off the highly skilled librarians can take up as your instructors and guides. Don't hesitate to ask for their help—the most sophisticated scholars do so every day. It will be given gladly and well.

General Description of The New York Public Library
What And Where Is The New York Public Library?

Ask a passerby in New York City where the Library is and chances are he will reply, "Oh, that's the place with the lions over on Fifth Avenue." Right. And wrong. For despite popular belief, the Central Building is not **the** Library, but is simply the biggest, most widely-known unit in a sprawling complex of libraries covering Manhattan, the Bronx, and Staten Island (Brooklyn and Queens have their own separate systems). Together, all the units of the network, sheltering under the title "The New York Public Library," combine to form one of the largest, most treasure-laden public library systems in the world. To be more accurate, The New York Public Library might better be called The New York Public Libraries.

The Circulating Or Branch Libraries

Within its interborough network the Library has two kinds of facilities: circulating and research. The circulating or Branch Libraries, numbering over 80, form the great bulk of the system. **Their materials, for the most part, may be borrowed for home use.**

The branches range from small neighborhood units, with relatively limited collections, to much larger installations, with extensive reference and circulating collections, such as the Mid-Manhattan Library—the Branch System's central library and the biggest and most diversified of all branches; the Borough Library Centers; and the strategically placed Regional Libraries. Occasionally, however, even a modest-seeming local branch, finely tuned to its neighborhood's special needs, will show surprising strength in a particular subject. The boating collection at the City Island Branch is a good example of this.

Of particular note is the General Library & Museum of the Performing Arts at Lincoln Center. Its collections, specializing in theatre, music, and dance are unique among circulating libraries. Another unusual branch is the Library for the Blind and Physically Handicapped. It circulates books and magazines in braille, on records and on tape by post-free mail to people who cannot read regular print because of a visual or physical handicap.

The Research Libraries

There are four Research Libraries. Though outnumbered twenty to one by the branches, they vigorously compensate for this by the size and magnificence of their collections. Among them, these great archives house over 5 million volumes, with materials in more than 3,000 languages and dialects—an awesome array of treasures, in which almost every imaginable subject is pursued to its smallest detail, and which draw scholars from every part of the world.

The Research Libraries are (1) the Central Building, whose more than eighty miles of shelves hold the accumulated records of man's knowledge in nearly every field; (2) the Annex, with its outstanding newspaper and patents collections; (3) the Schomburg Center for Research in Black Culture, perhaps the finest resource anywhere for black studies; (4) the Performing Arts Research Center at Lincoln Center, with collections of tremendous depth in theatre, music, and dance.

The collections of The Research Libraries are available to anyone who is eighteen or older (with the exception of certain restricted materials like the Special Collections in the Central Building), although they are suited mainly to the needs of scholars, advanced students, and specialists. Unlike the materials of The Branch Libraries, those of The Research Libraries **do not circulate,** but must be used within the library buildings.

Creatures of philanthropy, The Research Libraries depend heavily on endowments and contributions for their support.

What Is For Whom In The Library?

The New York Public Library, being truly public, serves everyone, from the toddler at his picture book hour to the scholar at his tome, and as soon as a person can write his name he is eligible for a borrower's card and may begin to take books home. However, for the mutual benefit of both toddler and scholar, and for all those in between, most Library facilities are designed to serve particular kinds of users, based on age, interests, and needs.

Children below the eighth grade who wish to go beyond the materials in their local branch will find in the Central Children's Room at Donnell Library Center one of the country's largest and finest collections of children's literature. Teenagers, from eighth grade through high school, have as their own special preserve, in addition to their local branches, Donnell's Nathan Straus Young Adult Library. It has a superb collection of books and magazines keyed to young people's interests.

For undergraduate college students and adults doing research below the postgraduate level, the Library offers a variety of options starting at the neighborhood branches and working up through the Regional Libraries and Borough Library Centers to the summit of the Branch System, the Mid-Manhattan Library. Mid-Manhattan's extensive collections will in most cases be able to satisfy reference and research requirements up to a very sophisticated level.

The same is true for the General Library & Museum of the Performing Arts in its special fields.

Beyond these lie the Research Libraries, whose riches especially await those who are doing original research or making an extremely intensive study of a subject.

In rare cases when a needed volume is missing or lacking in the collections, The Research Libraries — with perhaps a fleeting moment of chagrin — will try to borrow it from various research and academic libraries throughout the country.

Administrative Offices

In using the Library there may be times when you will have to make special arrangements through one or another of its Administrative Offices. For instance, in order to gain access to restricted materials in The Research Libraries — such as the Special Collections in the Central Building — you must first have permission from the Administrative Office of the unit in which the materials are housed. The same is true for using special study areas and typewriters. Reproduction of printed or illustrative materials for commercial purposes must also be cleared through the appropriate Administrative Office. The offices you will be most concerned with are these:

For the Central Building and Annex — Room 214, Central Building, Fifth Avenue and 42nd Street, New York, N.Y. 10018

For the Performing Arts Research Center at Lincoln Center — Room L-513, Library and Museum of the Performing Arts, 111 Amsterdam Avenue, New York, N.Y. 10023

For the Schomburg Center for Research in Black Culture — Information Desk, 103 West 135th Street, New York, N.Y. 10030

For the Branch Libraries — 6th Floor, Mid-Manhattan Library, 8 East 40th Street, New York, N.Y. 10016

Adult Education and Services

Although the Library does not offer courses of study for adults, it does provide a variety of stimulating programs throughout its branches. These include film showings, lectures, concerts, book discussion groups, dramatic and poetry readings, and exhibitions. Announcements of these activities, their locations and times, are given in **Events,** the bi-weekly Branch Libraries' publication. **Events** is available in all units and at the Inquiry Desk in the Central Building. The Readers' Adviser's Office in the Mid-Manhattan Library offers highly personalized reading guidance to adults. An individual's reading needs are discussed in depth, specific titles suggested, and book lists prepared. This service is primarily for recreational reading and is not for school or college assignments, or for professional researchers. Mid-Manhattan also has a selection of book and pamphlet materials covering public and private day and evening courses, correspondence courses, independent study programs, vocational training courses, reading lists, and financial aids to adults who wish to continue their education. Most branches have similar information on a more limited scale.

The Adult Services Office, 6th Floor, Mid-Manhattan Library, is responsible for coordinating policies and plans affecting adults and for maintaining high standards of service for adults throughout The Branch Libraries.

American History Division
Room 315A, Central Building

The materials of this Division are both vast and varied, offering scholars more than 125,000 volumes encompassing the history and pre-history of the New World (both North and South America). Here are found noteworthy collections on United States history generally, on black American history, and history of the Indians of the Americas. One of the Division's most interesting features is its outstanding collection of works in 300 Indian languages. Local histories of Canada, and Central and South America are also housed here. In addition to its books the Division has slides, stereopticon views, postcards, pamphlets, catalogs, political leaflets, immigration promotions, and speeches in vast number.

The Annex
521 West 43rd Street

A unit of The Research Libraries, the Annex houses the Newspaper Collection and Patents Collection. In addition, some infrequently used books from the Central Building are kept here. The catalog for these books is the Public Catalog in Room 315 of the Central Building. Consult it before you make a trip to the Annex.

Arents Collections
Room 324, Central Building

These two unique collections were founded and endowed by George Arents, Jr., pioneer in the development of cigarette manufacturing machinery. Each is probably the largest of its kind. The first, the Tobacco Collection, begins with rare books from 1507, and continues with other printed works, manuscripts, and pictorial documentation to the present, all concerned directly or indirectly with the history of tobacco. Included are important Americana, herbals, and significant works in American and English literature, and representative examples of early trade cards, cigar box designs, cigarette cards, and other ephemera.
The second, the Collection of Books in Parts, Mr. Arents defined as "works by an author which are published piecemeal over a period of time, each unit having its separate wrapper." Dickens is the most famous example of an author who issued his works in installments before the final bound edition, but many other subjects than novels also appeared in this form, particularly illustrated books.

Art and Architecture Division
Room 313, Central Building

This is The Research Libraries' major collection of history and design in the fine and applied arts—and one of the largest reference collections in these fields to be found anywhere. Architecture, painting, drawing, sculpture, costume, furniture, advertising art, crafts, and jewelry are among subjects thoroughly covered from ancient times to the present. (Graphic arts are located in the Prints Division, and engineering and building technology in the Science and Technology Research Center.) Scrapbooks and biographical dictionaries of artists are useful research tools. Major resources are the alphabetical clipping files on artists and institutions such as galleries, museums, and governmental agencies. Virtually unique in depth and comprehensiveness, the files include a great deal of hard-to-come-by early material. Art treasures to be found here include a set of original Piranesi etchings of architectural views; engravings of the fantastic building designs of Ledoux, the French visionary architect; and original French jewelry designs in the **art nouveau** style of the late nineteenth century. (See also Art Library)

Art Library
Donnell Library Center

The Branch Libraries' largest collection in the visual and graphic arts, and in related fields such as costuming, photography, handicrafts, printing, textile design, and advertising art will be found here. In addition to its approximately 11,000 books, the Art Library offers more than 70 American and foreign art periodicals, as well as reference files on contemporary artists and the trends they represent. Designed as both a circulating and reference collection for artists, students, and the general public, the Art Library is a companion to The Research Libraries' Art and Architecture Division.

Berg Collection
Room 320, Central Building

The Berg Collection of English and American Literature is one of America's most celebrated collections of first editions, rare books, autograph letters, and manuscripts. Presented to the Library in 1940 by Dr. Albert A. Berg, famous New York surgeon, in memory of his brother, Dr. Henry W. Berg, the Collection covers the entire range of English and American literature, with special emphasis on the 19th and 20th centuries. Represented by books and manuscripts are such English authors as Fanny Burney, Charles Dickens, William Makepeace Thackeray, George Bernard Shaw, and Virginia Woolf. Americans include Irving, Hawthorne, Melville, Thoreau, Whitman, Poe, Eugene O'Neill, and others. Material dealing with the Irish Literary Renaissance is another notable feature of the Collection. A spacious exhibition room (318) provides a pleasant public showcase for changing displays of the Collection's treasures and new acquisitions.

In order to use the Berg Collection, you must obtain a card of admission from Room 214.

Blind

The Library for the Blind and Physically Handicapped provides excellent services to people who cannot see or handle materials in regular print, and can refer readers to other collections throughout the Library as a whole, including collections of large print books. However, blind users of The Research Libraries who wish to bring their own readers should get in touch with the Administrative Offices of the unit in question so that arrangements can be made for access to materials.

Similar arrangements may be made in The Branch Libraries by talking with the head of the branch to be used.

b

Book Delivery System

Unlike books in The Branch Libraries, which you can usually pick out for yourself from the open shelves, those in The Research Libraries are kept in closed stacks and it is important to know how to get them. The book delivery system used in the Main Reading Room of the Central Building is used, with slight modifications, throughout The Research Libraries' various divisions and collections. This is how it works: the first step is to locate the item or items you want in the Public Catalog located in Room 315, or in the new Book Catalog. (Use the Public Catalog for materials cataloged before December 31, 1971, the Book Catalog for those cataloged since January 1, 1972.) Next, enter the catalog information onto call slips provided for the purpose, being very accurate in transcribing the class mark appearing on the upper right hand corner of the catalog cards or in the lower right hand corner of the Book Catalog entries. After completing a separate call slip for each title wanted, hand them in at the desk where it says "File Slips Here," and you will be given a card with a number on it. Now all you have to do is wait near the Main Reading Room's center enclosure for your number to appear in lights on the big indicator board as a signal that your books are available at the Delivery Desk.

When you have finished with your books please return them to that section of the Delivery Desk marked "Return Books Here."

Bookmobiles

Bookmobile service is provided on a regular basis in certain areas of the Bronx and Staten Island which are remote from a branch library. Books for adults, young adults, and children are brought by the bookmobile, and requests for special books may be given to the librarian. For schedules of bookmobile service in the Bronx call 933-5200; for Staten Island call 442-8611.

Borough Library Centers

A Library Center is the largest branch library in each borough, offering extensive reference, advisory, and lending services. They are as follows: in the Bronx, The Fordham Library Center; in Richmond, The St. George Library Center; in Manhattan, The Donnell Library Center. Donnell is exceeded in size only by the Mid-Manhattan Library, which is not considered a Library Center, but rather the central library of the Branch Library System.

Borrower, Non-resident

If you live outside New York State, you may borrow books from any of the Library's branches with your unexpired hometown library card. Or you may obtain a one-year non-resident borrower's card. There is no charge for children through the seventh grade. However, there is a small fee for adults.

If you live in Brooklyn or Queens, your Borough Public Library cards will be honored, although you are requested to register for a New York Public Library card. Your Brooklyn or Queens card may be used on the day of registration with full borrowing privileges.

Borrower's Card

A borrower's card is essential in order to borrow materials from The Branch Libraries. If you live, work, or attend school in New York State, and are old enough to write your name, you're entitled to one without charge.

Apply for your card at any branch library in Manhattan, the Bronx, or Staten Island by giving your name and address, and appropriate identification. Your card will be mailed to you. Meanwhile, a temporary card will be issued on which you may borrow two items at a time from the branch at which you applied. If you lose your card, report it at once by filling out a special form at any branch library. Until you do this you are financially responsible for all material borrowed on your card, with or without your consent. To obtain another card, you'll have to fill out a new application and pay a small fee.

Report a change in your name or address to any branch library, and a corrected card will be issued.

To insure uninterrupted borrowing privileges, re-register within three months of the expiration date on your card. After this period you'll be asked to furnish current identification when you register. Any commercial or research organization or welfare institution located in New York City may secure an organization borrower's card by obtaining an application at any branch library.

Borrowing Books, Periodicals and Records

Once you've received your regular borrower's card, you may borrow any reasonable amount of material from any branch (if you take out enough to fill a U-Haul, you'll probably be politely questioned).

Books and circulating periodicals are issued for 28 days, for shorter periods if they're in popular demand. Records usually circulate for two weeks, pictures for 28 days.

Duplicate copies (pay duplicates) of popular books and records are available in many branches for a modest daily rental fee plus sales tax.

Reference materials are for use only within the branch building. In most branches you may reserve a book by buying a stamped postcard which will be mailed to you when the book is available. Library materials may be returned to any branch with the exception of records, films, and pictures, which must be returned to the branch from which they were borrowed. There is a small charge for each day an item is kept beyond its due date.

Branch Libraries

The Branch Library System is the circulating arm of the Library, lending books, periodicals, films, recordings, and pictures for home use. With more than 80 units dotting Manhattan, the Bronx, and Staten Island, the System's diverse materials are convenient and accessible to great numbers of people. The branches range in the size and depth of their collections from the smaller neighborhood units to the Regional Libraries, which are larger, strategically located branches, to the Borough Library Centers, the largest branches in each borough. (However, Donnell, the Library Center for Manhattan, is exceeded in size by the Mid-Manhattan Library.) The Library Centers provide extensive reference, advisory, and lending services. The Mid-Manhattan Library, headquarters and central library of the System, with 375,000 books on open shelves and 1,033 seats for readers, is the largest, most comprehensive of all the branches. The General Library & Museum of the Performing Arts at Lincoln Center is unique in character for a circulating library and deserves special notice. Its large circulating and reference collections are devoted to theatre, dance, and music in all their aspects.

Beyond its function as a lending and reference source, The Branch Library System offers a tremendous variety of programs and activities for people of all ages—everything from story hours, pre-school programs, and films for the smallest children to poetry readings, concerts, films, lectures, book discussions, plays and more for teenagers and adults. The Branch Libraries are publicly supported, receiving most of their funds from the City and State of New York.

C

Call Slips

Despite their unassuming appearance, call slips are absolutely vital, because you cannot secure a book from The Research Libraries without one. Here is how to use them: blank slips are located in boxes on tables adjacent to the catalogs. Simply fill out the blanks including the correct bibliographical information from the catalogs and file them at that part of the central desk that says "File Call Slips Here." Ordinarily, no more than three slips may be filed at one time, although additional slips usually may be filed at intervals after the initial request.

Call slips are also used in the Mid-Manhattan Library and in Borough Library Centers for unbound periodicals, microform materials, and books not in open shelf areas.

Cards of Admission and Passes

To safeguard the rare and unique materials of The Research Libraries' Special Collections against excessive and unnecessary handling, a card of admission is required in order to use them. You may apply for one at the Administrative Office, Room 214, Central Building, by supplying personal identification and proof of research needs. Students must be engaged in degree programs of graduate study.

Most undergraduate research needs can be met by the Mid-Manhattan Library or the General Library & Museum of the Performing Arts at Lincoln Center. If, however, you are under eighteen and need to use The Research Libraries, you must ask for a pass from a librarian at Mid-Manhattan or at the General Library & Museum of the Performing Arts.

Catalog—Book (Research Libraries)

On January 1, 1972, The Research Libraries' card catalog system was officially phased out in favor of the less cumbersome, easier to use Book Catalog. As a result, all titles with 1972 imprint dates, and all other materials now being added to the collections, regardless of publication dates, are included in the Book Catalog and do not appear in the card catalogs.

The Book Catalog (or **Dictionary Catalog**) is produced by a computer processing system and is kept up to date on a monthly basis with supplements. The Catalog follows a dictionary form with arrangement of authors, titles, and subject headings in one alphabet, from A through Z. The Catalog includes books in all languages, with non-Roman alphabets appearing in romanized form. It also contains entries for books of maps, manuscripts in microform, and books of prints. Not included are individual sheet maps, original manuscripts, and individual prints.

Call numbers are located at the end of each entry and are identified by heavy brackets. When requesting materials for use you must supply the entire bracketed notation on your call slip.

There is considerable hope around the Library that the entire Public Catalog, consisting of more than 10 million cards, will some day be put into book catalog form.

Catalog—Book (Branch Libraries)

The Branch Libraries put their Book Catalog into effect in November, 1972, using as a base the Book Catalog prepared for the opening of Mid-Manhattan Library late in 1970. The Book Catalog supplants card catalogs for all materials added to the collections in branches since November 1972. (Mid-Manhattan Library and several new branches have no card catalogs.)

Unlike that of The Research Libraries, The Branch Libraries' Book Catalog treats titles, authors, and subject headings in separate volumes labeled "Titles," "Names," and "Subjects."

A key to book locations is a valuable feature of the Catalog. Symbols provided with each entry tell you in which department of Mid-Manhattan or in which of the largest branches your book may be found.

Children's books acquired since June 1972 have their own Book Catalog of titles, names, and subjects.

Both adult and children's book catalogs are updated with cumulative supplements.

Catalog—Public
Room 315, Central Building

Despite competition from the more contemporary, computerized Book Catalog, the main Public Catalog, with over 10 million cards, continues to hold its own as The Research Libraries' primary tool for retrieving materials. The Public Catalog lists items cataloged for The Research Libraries to the end of 1971 (items added to The Research Libraries' collections from January 1972 on are listed only in the Book Catalog), including books, periodicals, government documents, pamphlets, and microform materials using the Roman or Greek alphabets. It does not include cards for individual maps, individual prints, music scores, and manuscripts, or for books and periodicals using Cyrillic script, or for those in the Hebrew alphabet, or in Oriental languages.

The Public Catalog is a dictionary catalog with author, subject, and distinctive title entries filed in a single sequence. The staff at the Information Desk in Room 315 will be happy to assist you in using the Catalog.

Catalog—Union
Telephone 790-6234

This handy service will give you by phone the location of specific books and recordings in The Branch Libraries.

Catalogs—Divisional

Each subject division of The Research Libraries has its own card catalog. Materials listed in these are also listed in the main Public Catalog in Room 315. Some divisions also maintain special files and indexes of fugitive or ephemeral materials (clippings and scrapbooks, for example) to be found there, and these are not duplicated in the Public Catalog.

Catalogs of the Jewish, Oriental, and Slavonic Divisions include cards for materials in non-Roman alphabets, which will not be found in the Public Catalog.

Catalogs—Special Collections

The Special Collections of The Research Libraries maintain their own catalogs, and listings of the bulk of their holdings up to the end of 1971 do not appear in the main Public Catalog. However, all books (but not manuscripts) added to the Special Collections since January 1972 are included in the Book Catalog of The Research Libraries. Copies of Special Collections Catalogs are available for consultation in Room 315.

Central Building
Fifth Avenue and 42nd Street

The Central Building is one of the world's great archives. Its more than eighty miles of shelves embrace the accumulated records of what man has known and done, knows and does, in nearly every field of learning and endeavor. Its treasures, which include the Gutenberg Bible, the five First Folios of Shakespeare, and the handwritten copy of Washington's Farewell Address, attract scholars and researchers from everywhere. (The Central Building also draws sightseers from everywhere. The **Guide Michelin** for New York City stars it as a tourist attraction.)

The Central Building is the hub of The Research Libraries, housing by far the greatest number and diversity of collections as well as the Public Catalog, the primary index of The Research Libraries' holdings. It is also a museum, for its great halls and long corridors are lined with exhibits, both permanent and changing, of rare or outstanding items from the collections.

The magnificent building, built largely of Vermont marble, was designed by architects Carrère and Hastings and was opened to the public in 1911 after nine years of construction. It is now a National Historic Landmark and a New York City Landmark. Patience and Fortitude, the two famous lions doing sentry duty at the Fifth Avenue entrance, were carved of pink Tennessee marble by E.C. Potter.

Central Children's Room. (See **Donnell Library** and **Children's Services)**

Children's Services

Nothing is too good for the children as far as the Library is concerned, and much time, thought, and energy go into making its facilities stimulating and enjoyable places for youngsters to be. Nearly every branch has a room for children with collections of books for pleasure and study. Major lending collections of musical, non-musical recordings and cassettes are available in the children's rooms of the Borough Library Centers and the Library & Museum of the Performing Arts at Lincoln Center; smaller collections are in most other branches as well. Programs for children include story hours, picture book hours, pre-school programs, films, and sometimes special events such as plays, puppet shows, arts and crafts workshops. The Central Children's Room in Donnell Library Center, is the Library's largest children's collection. It has nearly 80,000 titles, including the best in many foreign languages and an extensive collection of rare and old books. Non-book materials consist of paintings and drawings by well-known children's book illustrators, paintings by children throughout the world, and a collection of old valentines. An exhibition of books listed in the Library's publication **Children's Books**

Suggested as Holiday Gifts takes place from late November through December. The publication may be picked up throughout the year at any children's room. Although designed primarily for children from pre-kindergarten through seventh grade, the Central Children's Room collection is extremely valuable to children's book writers and other adults interested in children's literature. The Children's Room at the General Library & Museum of the Performing Arts at Lincoln Center has a large collection of books relating to all phases of the performing arts, for children and adults working with children in these areas. There are permanent exhibits of puppets and marionettes from many Oriental lands, and memorabilia of Broadway's first child star, Elsie Leslie. The unique non-circulating listening collection of musical and non-musical recordings and cassettes recommended for children deserves special mention.

The James Weldon Johnson Memorial Collection is a rich and valuable source of children's books about the black experience. The Collection is kept on permanent reserve for use in the Children's Room of the Countee Cullen Regional Library, but most of the titles are available for circulation in Countee Cullen and in other children's rooms throughout the system. The Children's Services Office, 6th Floor, Mid-Manhattan Library, is responsible for upholding the quality of children's materials and services.

Circulation Division. (See Branch Libraries)

Civil Service

If you're interested in a civil service position, especially in New York City, the Library can help you on your way. All branch libraries have pre-application forms for New York City open competitive civil service examinations. Mid-Manhattan Library, the Borough Library Centers, and certain Regional Libraries have the following material for reference use: current announcements of examinations for some federal and state positions and all municipal positions; study manuals for specific examinations; civil service newspapers. In addition, Mid-Manhattan has a selective file of municipal promotional examinations. Some branches have circulating copies of the more popular study manuals.

College Catalogs

You'll find the most comprehensive collection of current catalogs of accredited American universities, colleges, and junior colleges in the Mid-Manhattan Library. Coverage of selected foreign universities is included as well.
Fordham Library Center and the St. George Library Center have current catalogs for selected colleges and universities throughout the country. Regional libraries and some smaller branches maintain reference collections of current catalogs, primarily for local schools. The Research Libraries do not keep current catalogs, but certain selected back files of leading American and foreign colleges and universities are on hand at the Annex.

Conservation of the Collections

As The Research Libraries are archival in nature, nearly all of their titles are represented by single copies, which are often difficult if not impossible to replace. Conservation of the collections is therefore vital. Overall responsibility for this falls to the Conservation Division, which is constantly engaged in physical restoration, binding, and rebinding as well as in preserving the intellectual content of materials through appropriate reproduction processes.
Conservation really begins at the users' level, however, and you are urged to handle materials with extreme care. Please bring those which appear to be in need of rebinding or other repair to the attention of a librarian.

Copyright

In photocopying, all responsibility for questions of copyright must be assumed by the user. The Library will not reproduce copyrighted material beyond recognized "fair use" without signed authorization of the copyright owner.
(See also Photographic Service)

a

Dance Collection
Performing Arts Research Center at Lincoln Center

This outstanding research collection is the world's largest
and most varied archive devoted solely to the dance. The
Collection has books, manuscripts, periodicals, films,
original costume and set designs, drawings, taped
interviews, scrapbooks, programs, clippings, posters,
letters, and memorabilia in many languages.
Every aspect of dance is covered: theatrical, historical,
educational, religious, and therapeutic. Every type of dance
is documented: ballet, modern dance, social, ethnic, folk,
and primitive. Here a reader can reconstruct an Elizabethan
court dance, a nineteenth century Italian tarantella, or a
Ceylonese devil dance of the twentieth century. One can
read the correspondence and exchange of telegrams that
form an account of Nijinsky's split with Diaghilev; learn the
problems Picasso faced in working on the ballet **Parade**
from letters in his own hand; or compare the modern dance
of Isadora Duncan with that of Denishawn, Martha Graham,
and Doris Humphrey.
The heavily used Jerome Robbins Film Archive, with its
tremendous collection of films of every kind of dancing, and
the Oral Tape Archive, with interviews of prominent people
in the profession, deserve special mention.
(See also General Library & Museum of the Performing Arts
at Lincoln Center)

Donnell Library Center
20 West 53rd Street

When Ezekiel J. Donnell, a successful Irish-émigré cotton
merchant, died in 1896, he bequeathed an estate to be
used for the construction of a library building "in which
young people can spend their evenings profitably away
from demoralizing influences." With this bequest the
Donnell Library Center was built in 1955 by The New York
Public Library. True to its donor's wishes, Donnell today
offers the Library's most extensive service to children and
young adults through its Central Children's Room and
Nathan Straus Young Adult Library. (See also Children's
Services, Young Adult Services.) As the Borough Library
Center for Manhattan it also has large collections of
circulating and reference books for adults and several
specialized collections. These are found in Donnell's various
departments: the Art Library, the Film Library, the Foreign
Language Library, the Record Library, the Reference
Library.
In its auditorium Donnell offers a wide diversity of programs.
An impressive variety of concerts, lectures, dramatic
presentations, poetry readings, and film showings takes
place regularly for persons of all ages without charge.

Economic and Public Affairs Division
Room 228, Central Building

The Division collects just about everything that relates to man's economic, social, and political activities, and does it so thoroughly that it has over a million volumes, making it one of The Research Libraries' largest divisions. Holdings are particularly strong in finance, advertising, marketing, labor, demography, and government. Business periodicals and journals abound and the Division's collection of government documents is one of the most comprehensive in existence. This includes official publications of international agencies and of individual nations at the federal, state, provincial, and local level.

Events

Events, a bi-weekly publication of The Branch Libraries, announces what's going on around the branches, where and when. Keep an eye on it for activities such as lectures, book discussions, dramatic and poetry readings, concerts, and film programs. Exhibitions taking place in the branches and in the Central Building are also listed. You can pick up a copy at any branch or at the Inquiry Desk in the Central Building.

Exhibitions

Holdings as rich and diverse as the Library's deserve to be shown off from time to time, and so the Library is also a museum, with exhibitions constantly taking place.
The Great Hall at the Fifth Avenue entrance of the Central Building is the location of major exhibitions, which usually continue on the staircase landings. Other exhibition areas in the Central Building include the first floor south corridor where Albrecht Dürer's **Triumphal Arch of Maximilian** and **The Development of Printing Types** are both on permanent display; the center corridor of the second floor for various changing exhibits; Room 318 in which the Berg Collection has changing exhibitions; and sliding frames on both sides of the Inquiry Desk, in which the Miller Collection of U.S. postage stamps is displayed. In addition, individual divisions often prepare their own exhibits, which are displayed in or adjacent to their rooms.
The Library & Museum of the Performing Arts at Lincoln Center holds regular exhibits in the Shelby Cullom Davis Museum, which includes the Plaza, Main, Amsterdam, and Vincent Astor Galleries. In addition, each division and collection mounts exhibitions in its own area. On display at the Schomburg Center for Research in Black Culture are African objects of ivory, metal, and wood, including the Eric de Kolb collection of African weaponry.
Exhibitions of various kinds are held in the branches.
Consult **Events** for subjects, locations, and dates.

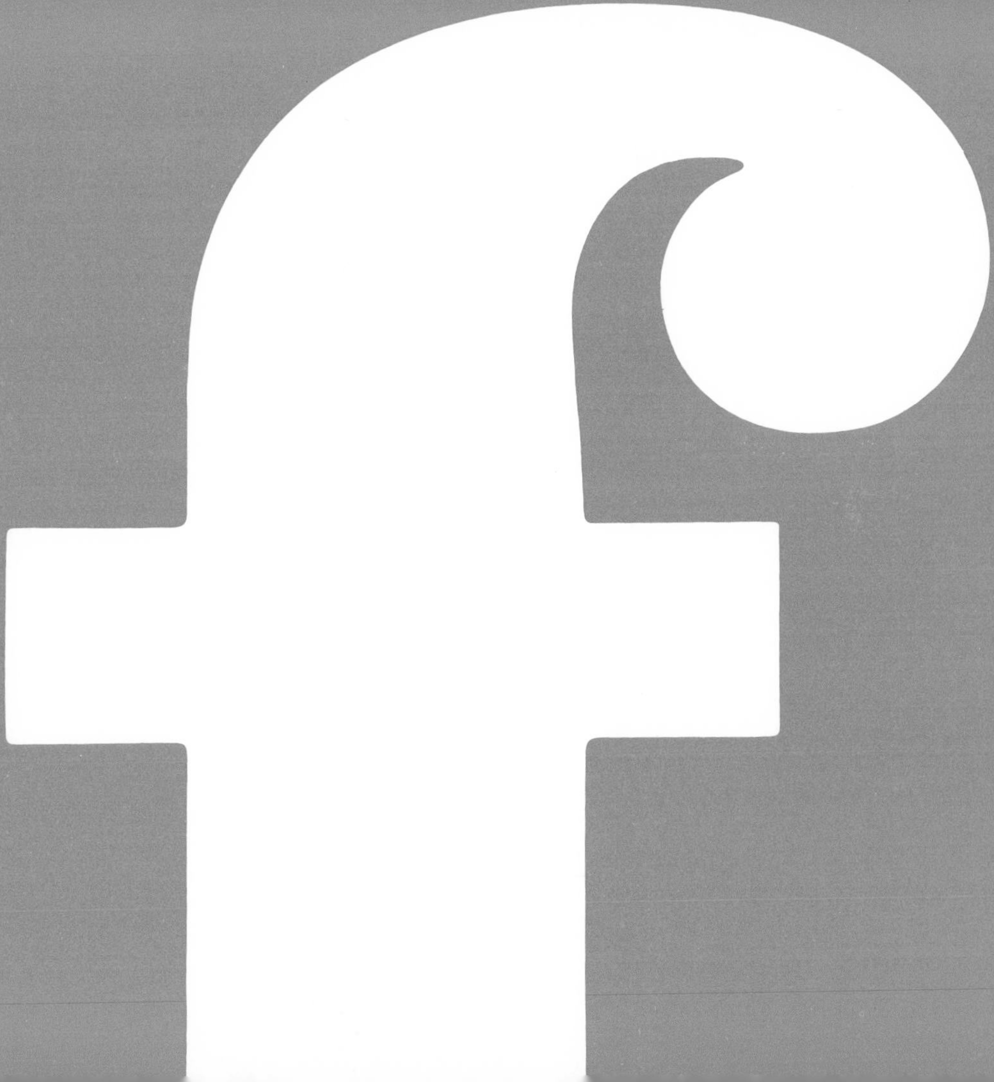

Films

For film buffs and scholars alike, the Library has excellent resources—both in reference materials and in actual films. The Film Library at Donnell Library Center has a collection of over 2,000 sixteen millimeter non-theatrical sound films carefully selected by library specialists for their particular interest to various age groups. The films are available for lending to individuals and non-profit organizations, but not to schools. The staff offers assistance in program planning, information, and reference services.

The General Library & Museum of the Performing Arts at Lincoln Center provides books, periodicals and pamphlets on films, and a few recordings of screenplays. Although primarily a circulating collection for students, buffs, and film-makers (it doesn't circulate films), it also has a good reference collection of all major works published in the field. Periodical holdings are indexed for articles of major interest. Newspapers and periodicals are clipped for reviews, which are filed by title in the cinema section of the file.

The Theatre Collection of the Performing Arts Research Center houses The Research Libraries' great collection on films. In addition to a file of film periodicals dating back to the industry's infancy, the Collection includes thousands of stills; pressbooks; files on film actors, directors, producers; and cinema scripts and other memorabilia.

The Dance Collection of the Performing Arts Research Center collects retrospective and current films of the dance.

Fordham Library Center
2556 Bainbridge Avenue, Bronx

This is the largest public library in the Bronx. It has a strong general collection, a sizeable collection of recordings, and a large collection of books on education.

The Bronx Reference Center, housed in the same building, has, in addition to basic reference tools, sizeable holdings in business; local history; college catalogs; vocational information; civil service; and periodicals, including **The New York Times** from 1851 on microfilm.

Foreign Languages — Branch Libraries

A Library serving the people of New York City, where in many districts English is a foreign tongue, has to be up on its languages, which the Library surely is.

The Donnell Foreign Language Library has a major circulating collection representing the literature of eighty or more languages. The largest of these collections are French, German, Italian, Russian, Spanish, Hungarian, Japanese, Polish, and Hebrew. Also available are books in Dutch, Norwegian, Yiddish, modern Greek, Chinese, Arabic, Gaelic, Hindi, Portuguese, and Swahili. There are a substantial number of foreign reference books and periodicals, and a staff of specialists in various languages to help readers in their use.

The Central Children's Room at Donnell has approximately 8,000 books in 50 languages. Collections of children's books in foreign languages are available in most branch children's rooms.

Mid-Manhattan Library has foreign language encyclopedias in French, German, Italian, and Spanish and dictionaries for many foreign languages. Mid-Manhattan's Literature and Language Department, located in the Central Building, has broad coverage of materials for the study and teaching of major and minor European, Asian, and African languages. Dictionaries and basic literary criticism in French and Spanish and also reference material on Puerto Rican literature, much of it in Spanish, are found in this department. A sizeable Spanish Collection on Puerto Rico is located in the History and Social Science Department. Significant foreign language collections are also located in the following branches:

Chinese	Chatham Square, Seward Park
Czech	Webster
French	Bloomingdale
German	Bloomingdale, Ottendorfer
Hebrew	Seward Park
Polish	Tompkins Square
Spanish	Aguilar, Hamilton Fish Park, High Bridge, Hunt's Point, Melcourt, Melrose, Morrisania, Mott Haven, Tremont, West Farms, Woodstock
Ukrainian	Tompkins Square
Yiddish	Seward Park

Foreign Languages—Research Libraries

Published materials in all languages are collected by The Research Libraries. Those in non-Roman alphabets and in Oriental languages are housed in the language divisions: Cyrillic materials in the Slavonic Division; Oriental languages, including Egyptian hieroglyphics, in the Oriental Division; Hebrew and Jewish materials in the Jewish Division. There are excellent collections in the Universal languages like Esperanto and in new official languages like Faroese and Macedonian. Little-known languages such as Basque, Celtic (including Manx and Cornish), and Sorbian are also collected. Materials in languages using the Roman alphabet will be found in the Public Catalog and Book Catalog.

General Library and Museum of the Performing Arts at Lincoln Center
111 Amsterdam Avenue

This is The Branch Libraries' facility at the Library's Lincoln Center installation (The Research Libraries' is the Performing Arts Research Center). It has broad circulating and reference collections in all areas of the performing arts.

Drama and dance are covered by books, periodicals, and clippings. Included are published plays and materials on theatre history and criticism, auditions, acting, cinema, radio, television, circus, puppets, costumes, stage design, and every form of dance, as well as materials on movement education, exercise, kinesiology, and dance instruction recordings.

Music is represented by scores of all periods and types, from folk to opera, vocal to orchestral. A circulating collection of scores and complete sets of parts is available to conductors and librarians of community orchestras. A large collection of books deals with all phases of music theory, history, composition, and performance. Newspaper and magazine clippings supplement the reference books and periodicals.

A first-rate collection of recordings is available for borrowing or playing in the library. It includes standard repertory in addition to new and unusual music, folk, jazz, popular music, plays, sound tracks, comedy monologues, and dialects.

The Children's Library provides youngsters with their own collections of books on the theatre, dance, music, puppetry, the circus, and cinema. Acting editions of children's plays, sheet music for children, recordings, and a listening area are also found here. The Heckscher Oval was especially designed for story hours and other programs.

The entire facility is most attractively housed in its contemporary Skidmore, Owings and Merrill interiors.

(See also Library & Museum of the Performing Arts at Lincoln Center)

General Research and Humanities Division
Room 315, Central Building

Being responsible for the largest number of subjects makes this The Research Libraries' busiest Division. Under its jurisdiction are general reference works, anthropology, archaeology, bibliography, biography, geography, history (except the Western Hemisphere), languages and literatures of the world (except those found in the Jewish, Slavonic, and Oriental Divisions), philosophy, printing, publishing, psychology, religion, sports.

The Division also administers the vitally important Public Catalog, which lists most of the millions of holdings in The Research Libraries up to the end of 1971. Here, too, are The Library of Congress catalog; bibliographies, including the Cumulative Book Index, which attempts to list all books published in the English language; various periodical indexes; the National Union Catalog, telling which books are held in libraries throughout the country; and the catalog of The British Museum, among others. The open shelf reference collection in the Main Reading Room comes under the Division's jurisdiction as well.

The expert staff will happily provide assistance in the use of the various catalogs and other research tools located in Room 315.

General Reference Service— Mid-Manhattan Library
4th Floor, 8 East 40th Street

This is The Branch Libraries' most concentrated gathering of general basic reference materials, covering almost every subject. Here you'll find reference books such as encyclopedias, indexes, and biographical dictionaries. In addition, there are national, trade, and subject bibliographies; periodical and newspaper indexes; directories, almanacs, statistical compilations, and other sources of quick information. On hand, too, are civil service manuals, general magazines, and newspapers. Some basic reference works on art, music, theatre, dance, and film will also be found here, although major collections in these fields are located in the Donnell Art Library and at the General Library of the Performing Arts.

Handicapped

Any special arrangements that are necessary for a physically handicapped user should be made through the Administrative Office of the building concerned.

People in wheelchairs should plan their visits to the Central Building in advance through the Administrative Office in Room 214, as there is no street level entrance at Fifth Avenue and 42nd Street. A wheelchair ramp is available for use at a side entrance, but building staff need to be on hand to put it in place.

The following branches have entrances without steps on street level that are suitable for wheelchairs:

Manhattan	Donnell, 58th Street, Hamilton Fish Park, Inwood, Kips Bay, Performing Arts (Plaza level), Mid-Manhattan
Bronx	Baychester, City Island, Eastchester, Edenwald, Jerome Park, Melcourt, Riverdale, Soundview, Spuyten Duyvil, Throg's Neck, Van Cortlandt, Van Nest-Pelham, Woodlawn Heights
Staten Island	Dongan Hills, New Dorp, Prince's Bay, St. George, South Beach, Todt Hill-Westerleigh

(See also Library for the Blind and Physically Handicapped)

History of The Library

The Library's roots go back to 1848, when the terms of John Jacob Astor's will established a reference library. The Astor Library opened in 1854 with 90,000 volumes. Another reference library, the Lenox Library, established by James Lenox, opened in 1870. In 1895, the Astor and the James Lenox Libraries were consolidated with the Samuel Jones Tilden Trust to form The New York Public Library, Astor, Lenox and Tilden Foundations. The Central Building, erected by the City of New York, opened in 1911 with 1.2 million volumes and 18 special subject reading rooms.

In 1901, following Andrew Carnegie's offer to the city of building funds, the Library also became responsible for the operation of the publicly supported Branch Library System, which now consists of more than 80 branches in the Bronx, Manhattan, and Staten Island.

History and Social Science Department— Mid-Manhattan Library
5th Floor, 8 East 40th Street

This is Mid-Manhattan's largest department, with depth in a wide number of fields. Among these are histories of all countries, with broad coverage of the United States, Europe, Asia, and Africa; biography; sociology and anthropology; ethnic studies; political science and law, including books on government, international relations, and urban affairs; psychology and education, both theory and methods, study guides for tests, course directories, 4,000 college catalogs; business, economics, and industrial relations, major business services, and current annual reports for 500 of the country's top corporations. In addition, a collection on public access television has recently been developed.

Hours the Libraries are Open

These can be elusive as they vary from facility to facility and from winter to summer. You can learn the current hours of any Library facility by calling Telephone Reference Service (790-6161).

Information Desk
Room 315, Central Building

Set amid the Public Catalog and other vital catalogs, indexes, bibliographies, and references, the Information Desk is the center of The Research Libraries as far as most researchers are concerned. It is here that the experienced librarians can tell the scholar how most effectively to use the Library and also what resources are available to him. These experts often know about materials which the scholar, on his own, might never reach through indexes and catalogs. Their assistance in research projects is invaluable. On a less lofty level, the librarians will happily help the layman in the use of any of the many research tools located in the room. The desk is manned by the staff of the General Research and Humanities Division.

Inquiry Desk
Fifth Avenue entrance, Central Building

The staff at the Inquiry Desk, just inside the Central Building's Fifth Avenue entrance, knows what's what and what's where around the Library. They will be happy to provide you with information about materials available, services offered by both The Research and The Branch Libraries, and the opening and closing hours of every facility.

Interlibrary Loans

When a book requested for reserve is not in the collection of the branch at which it was requested, every effort will be made to borrow it from another unit in The Branch Libraries System. If it cannot be found there it may, in certain cirumstances, be borrowed from another library in the city, state, or elsewhere in the country through state and national interlibrary loan networks.
The Research Libraries will also borrow for their readers when a needed volume is missing or lacking in the collections. Borrowing may take place through the New York State Interlibrary Loan network or from various research and academic libraries throughout the nation.
(See also Reserving Books)

Jewish Division
Room 84, Central Building

The Division's collection consists of material on the Jews
and all phases of their life and history in all languages, and
works in Hebrew, Yiddish, Ladino, and other Jewish dialects
on a variety of subjects. A book on Jewish philosophy in any
language would be here, as would a book in Hebrew on
aeronautics. Gems of the collection include two manuscript
festival prayer books, each two volumes on vellum, one from
the fourteenth century and one from the fifteenth, nearly
forty fifteenth-century printed books, including a copy on
vellum of Jacob ben Asher's Arba'ah Turim (Piove di Sacco,
1475), a legal code, one of the earliest books bearing a date
to be printed in Hebrew, and over a thousand books from
the sixteenth century. Modern phases of Jewish life are
represented widely and well in books and periodicals.
Newspapers, American and foreign, are available on
microfilm, but most current periodicals in the Roman
alphabet are in Room 108 (Periodicals Section). The Jewish
Division catalog lists all The Research Libraries' holdings in
any language dealing with Jewish subjects, as well as all of
their publications in Hebrew characters. The **Dictionary
Catalog of the Jewish Division** has been published in
book form. It will be supplemented.

1

Large Print Materials

Large print materials for people with limited sight are available for borrowing in most of the Library's branches. Books, newspapers, and magazines are included. Sizeable collections are located at the Popular Library of Mid-Manhattan, Donnell Library Center, Grand Concourse Regional Library, and St. George Library Center. The Office of Adult Services has information on the development and availability of large print materials.

Library and Museum of the Performing Arts at Lincoln Center
111 Amsterdam Avenue

Architecturally, this is the Library's handsomest facility. Its striking Saarinen-designed building, which also houses the Vivian Beaumont Theatre, was opened in 1965.
The Library & Museum of the Performing Arts has two separate and distinct facilities. The first, the General Library & Museum of the Performing Arts, is part of The Branch Libraries. It has large circulating and reference collections in music, dance, and drama, along with a recordings collection and a beautifully equipped Children's Library. The General Library & Museum occupies the ground, first, and second floors of the building.
The second facility, located on the third floor, is the Performing Arts Research Center. It belongs to the Research Library System and materials from its vast non-circulating holdings in every area of the performing arts are geared for use especially by scholars, advanced researchers, and professionals.
Interesting exhibitions are continuously on display in the Shelby Cullom Davis Museum, which consists of the Plaza Gallery, Main Gallery, Amsterdam, and Vincent Astor Galleries. Exhibits include treasures from the Performing Arts Research Center, such as autograph scores, original costume and set designs, letters, and memorabilia. The Library's auditorium is the scene of a variety of free programs for the public.

Library for the Blind and Physically Handicapped
166 Avenue of the Americas

The collection of this library consists of nearly 80,000 talking books (books and magazines recorded on discs and open reel tapes, and books on cassettes), 3,500 tapes, and 12,000 volumes of braille. It is provided by the Library of Congress as a postage-free mailing service to people who cannot see or handle materials in regular print and whose mailing address is New York City or Long Island.

A statement signed by a professional person (doctor, nurse, optometrist, librarian, social worker) briefly describing the reading disability is all that is necessary in order to use the Library's services. Once the statement is received the library mails the user a specially designed record player (talking book machine), catalogs of available titles, sample books and order forms. From then on, books and magazines requested are mailed on a regular basis. Specially trained librarians assist readers of all ages, parents, and teachers in selecting books. Other volunteers, employees of telephone company affiliates known as the Telephone Pioneers, maintain a repair service for the thousands of talking book machines in use by readers in the New York area.

Lincoln Center, The New York Public Library at. (See Library & Museum of the Performing Arts)

Literature and Language Department— Mid-Manhattan Library
Rooms 78 and 80, Central Building

This is the only department of Mid-Manhattan that's not located at 8 East 40th Street. The Department has two sections: the Popular Library and circulating books in Room 80; reference books and periodicals around the corner in Room 78.

The reference collection covers American and English literature, early to modern; foreign literature in translation; periodicals, including critical journals as well as a representative collection of little magazines; materials on history, theory, and teaching of language; guides for the study of 100 languages and dialects; records and cassettes for learning 25 languages.

The Popular Library offers popular books on popular subjects for loan—novels, plays, and nonfiction in greatest current demand. Over 25,000 paperbacks are also available. Phonograph records and cassettes for learning languages are available for circulation and reference.

Local History and Genealogy Division
Room 315G, Central Building

The collection includes the histories of counties, cities and towns in the United States, the British Isles, and the Republic of Ireland; family histories with emphasis on American families of European origin, coats of arms, flags, and books on the origin and meaning of personal and family names. The Division has a large collection of ephemeral materials concerning localities in the United States, pictorial scrapbooks of local views in the United States, postcard views of New York City, and some 50,000 mounted photographs of New York City street scenes. Current periodicals in the Division's several areas of interest are shelved here as are many local New York City community newspapers.

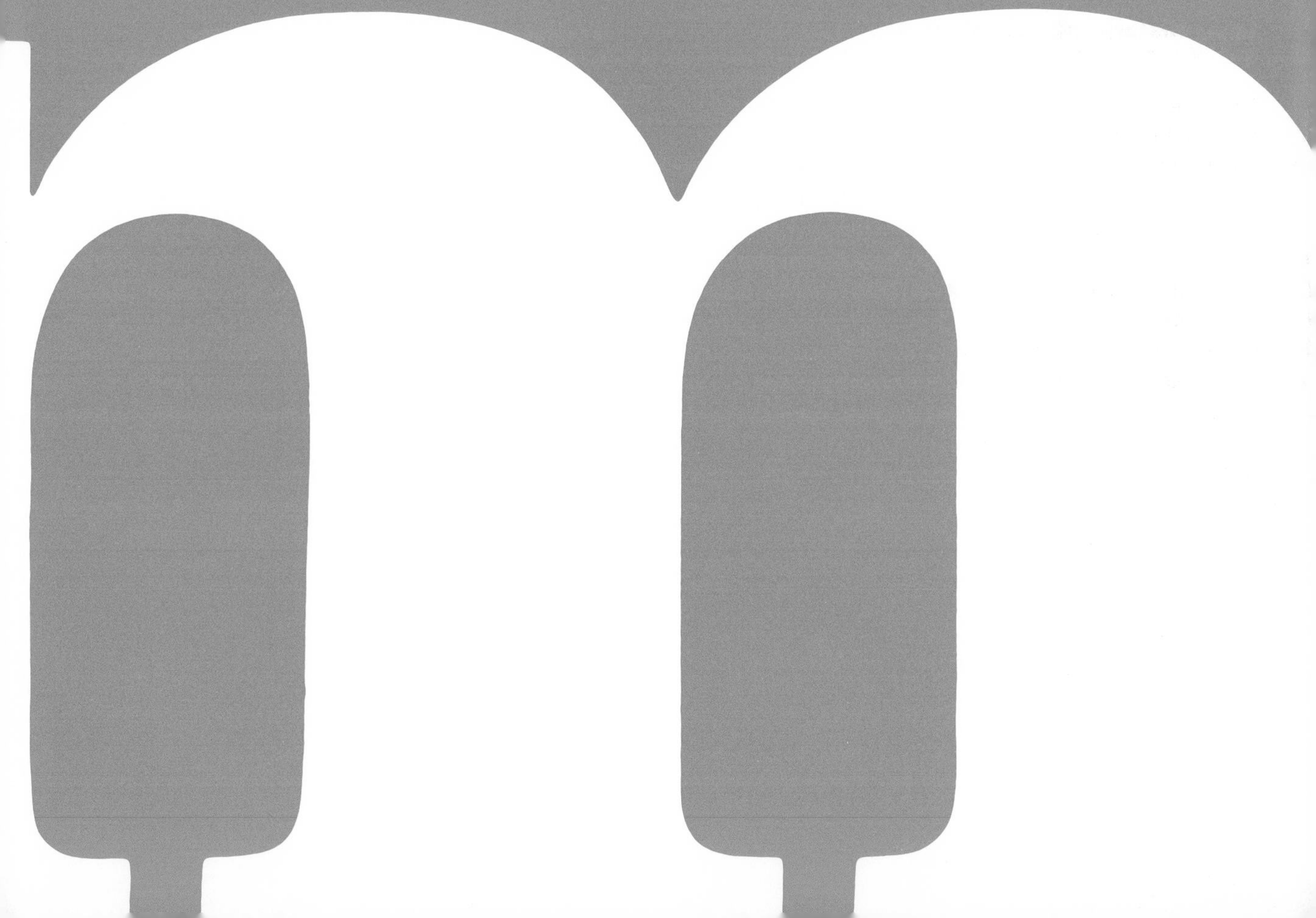

Main Reading Room
3rd Floor, Central Building

You will probably end up here—most people do—when you come to do research in the Central Building. The Main Reading Room is a magnificent hall (actually two halls, north and south) with tall arched windows and towering ceilings, that can seat 700 people without seeming crowded. A basic collection of about 35,000 reference books is kept on open shelves around the walls comprising considerable material in foreign languages, including the major foreign language dictionaries and encyclopedias. It also covers national and trade directories of American or European countries, a comprehensive selection of ready reference works, biography and history, and an especially extensive collection in literature. You may consult these freely or ask for help from the staff.

Manuscripts and Archives Division
Room 319, Central Building

This is The Research Libraries' largest collection of manuscripts. Whatever man has directly inscribed his message upon is collected here, and so the Division owns treasures among which are 5,000-year-old Babylonian clay tablets, Chinese scrolls, the **Farewell Address** in Washington's own hand, and an illuminated manuscript of Ptolemy's **Geography.** More contemporary manuscripts include Herman Melville's family letters and records and Theodore Dreiser's manuscript of **Sister Carrie.** Emphasis in recent years has been on building collections that reflect American political and social history, particularly of New York State and New York City. The catalog of the Division has been published in book form.
You must obtain a card of admission from the Administrative Office in order to use the materials of this Division.

Map Division
Room 117, Central Building

The most used public map room in the world, The Research Libraries' Map Division collects every conceivable cartographic item from rare early American and European maps to current road maps. Plans of American and foreign cities, maps of all countries, atlases, gazetteers, cartographic periodicals, and books on the history and making of maps can be found here in profusion. The materials are fascinating, the staff helpful. They've even been known to tell people how to get from midtown Manhattan to remote sections of Brooklyn. **The Dictionary Catalog of the Map Division** has been published in book form and will be supplemented.

Microform Reading Room
Room 315M, Central Building

This is the reading room for general microform reading materials in the stacks and for those divisions of The Research Libraries that do not have their own microform readers. These holdings are represented in the Public Catalog and Book Catalogs in Room 315. The Microform Reading Room has **The New York Times** from its first issue in 1851 to its latest microfilmed issue, along with films of some other New York City newspapers. Microfilm files of major American and foreign newspapers are housed in the Newspaper Collection at the Annex.

Microforms

With collections growing and storage space shrinking, microforms of all types are being increasingly used by the Library as a means to get great amounts of material into the smallest possible space. In the Central Building, apart from those in the Microform Reading Room, there are microform readers in the Economic and Public Affairs Division, and in the Jewish, Slavonic, and Oriental Divisions. There are also reading machines in the Annex, the Schomburg Center, and the Performing Arts Research Center.

Borough Library Centers have microfilm holdings of some newspapers and periodicals. Mid-Manhattan Library has extensive microfilm files in each department to supplement or duplicate bound materials and a growing collection of microfiche.

Mid-Manhattan Library
8 East 40th Street

The Mid-Manhattan Library, which opened in October 1970, is the central library of the Branch Library System. It occupies the fourth, fifth, and part of the sixth floor of its building (plus a few areas in the Central Building). Although designed primarily for undergraduate college students and business professional men and women who need a wide range of information for their studies or work (The Research Libraries serve scholars and those doing advanced research, and the high school student's own information center is the Nathan Straus Young Adult Library at Donnell), all who come to Mid-Manhattan are welcome. Mid-Manhattan has 375,000 books and over 36,000 bound volumes of periodicals on open shelves, and it offers the largest selection of books for home reading within The New York Public Library. As the major reference center for The Branch Libraries, however, it keeps almost half of its collection for use inside the building. In addition to encyclopedias, indexes, handbooks, and other reference works, one copy of nearly every important nonfiction book is kept for consultation. This means that even current books in great demand are always available in the library. Mid-Manhattan's collection of back issue periodicals is one of the largest on open shelves in the country and titles are listed separately in **Periodicals in the Mid-Manhattan**

Library. Current copies and back issues, bound in volumes and on microfilm, are located in all departments according to their subjects. Microfilm reader-printers and photocopiers make it easy to duplicate pages. The History and Social Science Department also has a microfiche reader-printer.

The library has four departments: General Reference Service; Science; History and Social Science; Literature and Language, including its Popular Library. All are located in the Library's own building except Literature and Language whose collections are two blocks away in Rooms 78 and 80 of the Central Building.

Other facilities offered by Mid-Manhattan are the Readers' Adviser's Office which helps readers select books and prepares reading lists; the Telephone Reference Service, which gives quick answers to questions on many subjects by phone; the Union Catalog, which gives, by telephone, the location of any book within The Branch Libraries.

Music Division
Performing Arts Research Center at Lincoln Center

The whole world of music is here, along with its literature, from the earliest notated stages to the latest electronic score. This great scholarly collection is one of the five or six largest music libraries in the world, and the varieties of access it provides to its collections are unique. Here are hundreds of thousands of musical scores and books on music; prints; photographs; letters; operatic scene designs; clipping files; and thousands of opera and concert programs. Of special note are the Americana Collection, with its broadsides, tunebooks, and sheet music collections ranging from rare 18th century American imprints to popular songs of recent generations, and the Toscanini Memorial Archives, with its growing collection of microfilms of the autograph scores of European composers. Other assets of the Division are early treatises, including over 20 incunabula, and musical autographs by such composers as Bach, Mozart, Brahms, and Stravinsky. Through a variety of special files, such as the song index, the program notes index, or the Black Music index, the Division provides in-depth access to its materials. In addition, an on-going series of concerts, exhibitions, publications, and special projects, such as the contemporary musical notation project, highlight important parts of the Division and make it an integral part of the performing arts community.
(See also General Library & Museum of the Performing Arts at Lincoln Center)

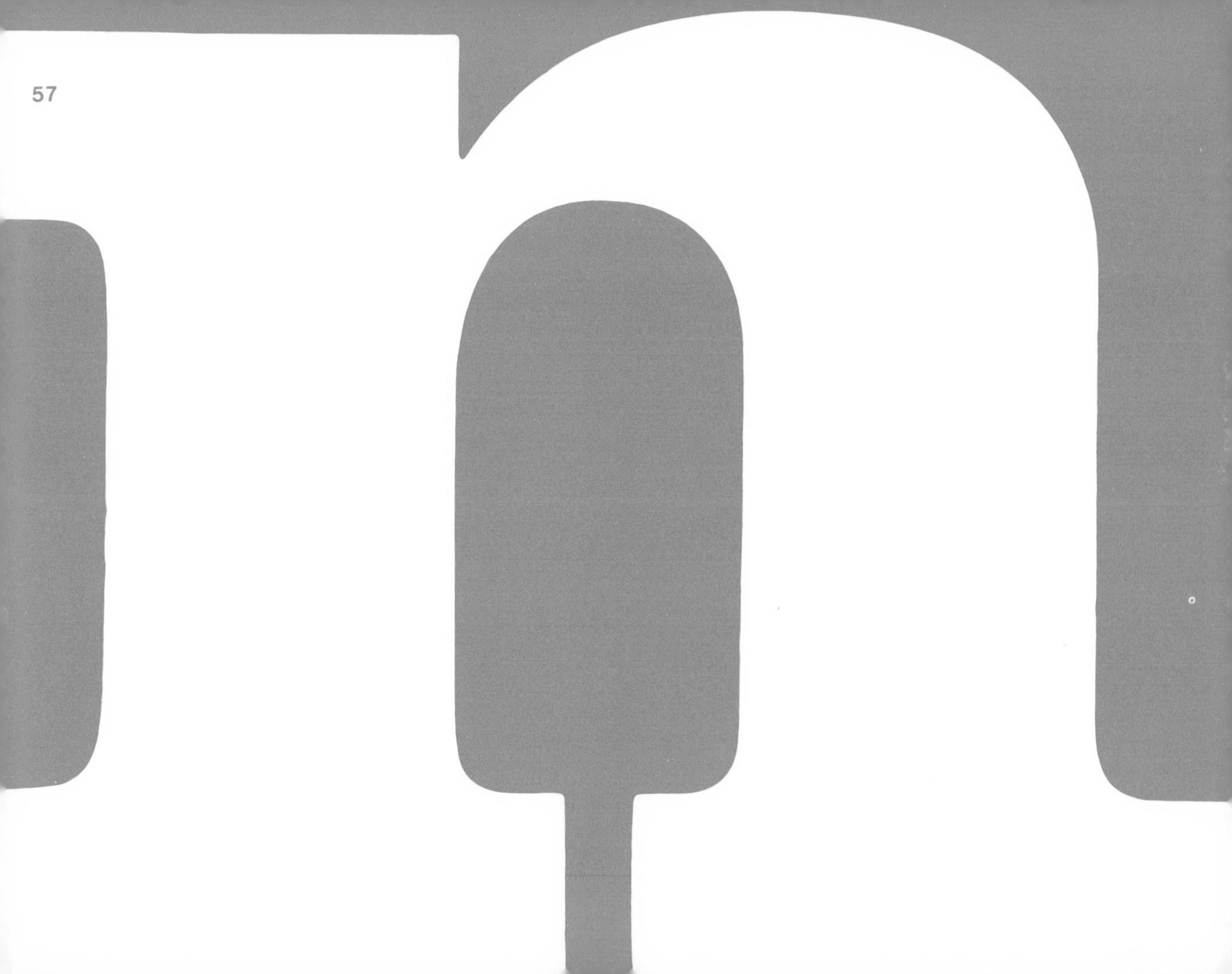

Nathan Straus Young Adult Library
(See Donnell Library and Young Adult Services)

Newspaper Collection
521 West 43rd Street

The Newspaper Collection is housed in the Annex, The Research Libraries' westernmost outpost. The Collection contains newspapers of many American and foreign cities, but not current ones, as the collection is primarily an archive. Microfilmed issues are available, however, usually a few months after publication. A complete catalog of newspaper titles available in The Research Libraries is here and also at the Information Desk, Room 315, Central Building. Jewish, Oriental, and Slavonic newspapers are cataloged and kept only in their own divisions. Eighteenth century American newspapers and other newspaper rarities are in the Rare Book Division. Current issues of several New York City local community newspapers are on file in the Local History and Genealogy Division.

Newspapers

The Research Libraries have back files rather than current issues of general daily newspapers, except for **The New York Times** and **Wall Street Journal.** Most branches, however, subscribe to one or more daily papers and to local neighborhood publications. Where local interest warrants, foreign language newspapers published in New York City are available in the branches. (See also **Periodicals—Branch Libraries; Foreign Languages—Branch Libraries** for language interests of the branches.) Borough Library Centers and Regional Libraries have back files of newspapers in the original or on microfilm. Mid-Manhattan's General Reference Service has files of **The New York Times** from 1851 on microfilm, and files of varying length of other major New York City publications. Foreign newspapers are not available in these locations except for **The Times,** London, 1914 to date, and current issues of the **Manchester Guardian** which are available in Mid-Manhattan. A few newspapers from major U.S. cities are also on hand, with a three-month back file.

Oriental Division
Room 219, Central Building

Thirteenth century Arabic medical books and current Japanese telephone directories are among the myriad things you'll find in The Research Libraries' Oriental Division. The Division collects materials throughout a huge portion of the earth, stretching from Morocco to the shores of Japan. Religion, literature, archeology, history, economics, politics, law and many other subjects are here in tongues ranging from Chinese to Kazak. Grammars and dictionaries of Oriental languages are an outstanding feature of the collection. (Hebrew is not included. See Jewish Division.) Some works dealing with Oriental matters in English and European languages are also housed here. The catalog in the corridor outside Room 223 lists all the Division's holdings as well as most of the works in other parts of the Library that are concerned with the Near, Middle, and Far East. The catalog has been published in book form.

O

Paintings and Sculpture

In addition to the portraits and busts of benefactors that all great institutions acquire, the Library owns some truly outstanding paintings. Most of these came along with the Lenox Library when it became part of The New York Public Library in 1895.

Some fine portraits by American masters hang in Room 318 of the Central Building, among them Gilbert Stuart (portraits of Washington and others), James and Rembrandt Peale (portraits of Washington), John Singleton Copley, and Samuel F.B. Morse (portrait of Lafayette). The room also contains portraits by Sir Joshua Reynolds, Augustus John, and others. Near the south end of the third floor's Central Hall hangs **Kindred Spirits** by Asher B. Durand. A masterpiece of the Hudson River School of Painting, it shows the artist Thomas Cole and the poet William Cullen Bryant in a Catskill Mountain landscape.

One of the most admired and touched pieces of sculpture in the Library is **Girl Crossing a Stream,** which is outside Room 73 in the Central Building. The piece came to the Library as part of the original Astor collection. The artist is unknown.

The Library does not purchase paintings and sculpture and is not adding to its collection. Gifts, to be acceptable, must be limited to portraits by prominent artists of sitters who have some official relation to the Library, or individuals eminent in literature, science, or the arts.

p

Pamphlets

The pamphlet collections of The Research Libraries, extending in depth from the seventeenth century to the present, are among their most treasured holdings. Pamphlets, often treated as throw-aways, are rarely granted the respect shown a book and therefore are frequently the hardest of materials to acquire and replace. In thousands of cases the Library's copy is the only one that survives. The Research Libraries' pamphlets are fully cataloged.
Most branches have pamphlet files of materials not readily found in the book collection. Pamphlets are usually for reference use only, but may sometimes be available for circulation.

Paperbacks

Paperbacks are collected for circulation by most branches. The Popular Library of Mid-Manhattan has the biggest collection. Its more than 25,000 paperbacks include many current titles and subjects in popular demand; also fiction and nonfiction in French and Spanish.

Patents Collection
521 West 43rd Street

Second only to that of the U.S. Patent Office is The Research Libraries' Patents Collection. Here's where patent attorneys and would-be Thomas Edisons search out patents foreign and domestic. The Collection has complete bound files of U.S. patents from 1872 to the present, the latter on a weekly basis, and brief abstracts all the way back to 1790. Complete, up-to-date files are here for British, French, German, Danish, and Swedish patents and abstracts for many other countries, as are books on patent law, patent and trademark forms.

Pay Duplicates

Many branches keep a duplicate collection of best sellers and currently popular books for a small daily rental plus sales tax. Pay duplicate books may not be reserved. Branches with record collections may also provide records on a pay duplicate basis. The rental is the same for an album as for a book.

Performing Arts Research Center at Lincoln Center
111 Amsterdam Avenue

This is The Research Libraries' performing arts facility, located in the splendidly designed Library & Museum of the Performing Arts at Lincoln Center. It has tremendous depth in nearly every area of the performing arts and is intended primarily for the professional, advanced student, and specialist. The Performing Arts Research Center is divided into the Theatre Collection, Dance Collection, Music Division, and the Rodgers and Hammerstein Archives of Recorded Sound. Treasures from the Center's collections are displayed in frequently-changing exhibitions in the Vincent Astor Gallery on the second floor of the building.

Periodicals—Branch Libraries

Borough Library Centers and Regional Libraries have more extensive files of periodicals for general reference use than other branches. Special collections in the branches have large numbers of periodicals related to their fields. The publication, **Periodicals in the Branch Libraries,** available in all branches, will give you individual titles, branches where they are held, and length of files. Some branch libraries circulate the more popular periodicals. At Mid-Manhattan, however, periodicals may be used only within the Library itself. Mid-Manhattan periodical holdings appear only in **Periodicals in the Mid-Manhattan Library.**

Periodicals Section
Room 108, Central Building

Unlike most components of The Research Libraries, the primary interest of Periodicals Section is the present. For its business is current periodicals — in the humanities, popular and professional journals, and the publications of trade and labor unions. The first room of the section handles foreign language publications, the second those in English. More specialized periodicals are located in The Research Libraries' various subject divisions. Non-current periodicals, bound in volumes, are available through Room 315 or the subject divisions. The Section's catalog lists all titles being currently received in The Research Libraries except those in the Cyrillic and Hebrew alphabets, and in Oriental languages. A second catalog lists all currently received periodicals by country of origin. All titles of American and foreign language periodicals in The Research Libraries that are no longer being published are entered only in the Public Catalog in Room 315 and in the various subject and language divisions.

Photocopying Facilities

Photocopying service is available for a fee at the Annex, at the Performing Arts Research Center, and at the Central Building for Library materials only. Coin-operated photocopiers are provided for reader use in the General Library and Museum of the Performing Arts, the Mid-Manhattan Library, and in many branches. Coin-operated readers-printers for photocopying microforms are also available at Mid-Manhattan.
The Branch Libraries do not have a copying service. All copying in the branches is strictly do-it-yourself on coin-operated machines.

Photographic Service
Room 316, Central Building

The Research Libraries' Photographic Service provides a copying service of Library materials only, at cost, by electrostatic methods, photography, photostat, or microphotography. Certain works may not be copied because of the danger of damage, because they are inappropriate for duplication or for other reasons. The Library reserves the right to refuse permission to reproduce materials.

All responsibility for questions of copyright must be assumed by the applicant, and copyrighted material will not be reproduced beyond recognized "fair use" without authorization of the copyright owner.

Picture Collection
Room 73, Central Building

This is the Library's largest pictorial archive, and it is organized both for reference and for loan. The collection has a core of nearly 2,000,000 pictures specially classified and indexed by subject. The clippings and photographs are arranged in large folders kept in open bins where you can search until you find what you're looking for. An outstanding feature of the collection is that the pictures are "sourced"—that is, each one has a key indicating where it was clipped from, so that a researcher can go to that source and read further if he wants. Advertising people, industrial designers, book illustrators, fashion designers, etc. love the place.

Incidentally, pictures may not be borrowed for school use or exhibitions, purposes for which they are not suitably mounted.

Picture Taking

Most facilities of the Library are accessible for photography and filming to members of the press, although it is advisable to phone in advance.

Motion picture filming, still photography, and the taking of slides for scholarly, personal, or study reasons may usually be performed without charge. All commercial photography and filming is subject to a fee. Arrangements, financial and otherwise, must be made in advance with the Press and Communications Office (The Branch Libraries) or with The Research Libraries' Administrative Office.

Photography in a unit should be discussed with the unit librarian so that permission may be cleared with the Branch Libraries' Press and Communications Office, or, in the case of The Research Libraries, with the Public Information and Public Relations Office, Room 221, Central Building.

Prints Division
Room 308, Central Building

This Special Collection of The Research Libraries houses an excellent representation of original prints from the fifteenth century to the present, supplemented by reference books and catalogs on individual printmakers as well as literature on the history and techniques of printmaking. The Division has approximately 150,000 original prints—and some drawings—which are arranged by artist rather than by subject (with some notable exceptions, among them the I.N. Phelps Stokes Collection of American Historical Views and the Eno New York City Views); Mary Cassatt, Edouard Manet, and Kitagawa Utamaro are among artists particularly well represented. Especially interesting and useful are the Prints Division's holdings of political caricatures, portraits, bookplates, and book illustrations.

In order to use the Prints Division you must have a card of admission from the Administrative Office.

Rare Book Division
Room 303, Central Building

The chief subject is Americana, particularly before 1800, of which the nucleus is the James Lenox collection. Other interests of Mr. Lenox were early Bibles, Shakespeare, Milton, Walton, and Bunyan's **Pilgrim's Progress.** Housed here are the following large categories of printed materials: European before 1601, English before 1641, American before 1801, and Latin American before 1801. Books after these dates depend on American interest and rarity. Examples are Confederate imprints, rare Mormon items, and first editions of significant English and American literary authors. Broadsides and miniature books (under four inches) are examples of other types of material included in this Division.

The large and rapidly growing collection of modern special and private press books includes those of the Ashendene, Grabhorn, Gregynog, Kelmscott, Merrymount, Overbrook, and many others. Books designed by such men as Bruce Rogers, John Henry Nash, and Frederic William Goudy are found here.

Reader-Printers

Reader-Printers are available in The Research Libraries at the following locations: **Central Building**—Microform Reading Room (315M), Photographic Services Room (316); **Performing Arts Research Center; Schomburg Center for Research in Black Culture.** Mid-Manhattan Library has coin-operated microfilm reader-printers in all of its departments and a microfiche reader-printer in the History and Social Science Department.

Readers' Adviser
Mid-Manhattan Library

The Readers' Adviser's Office offers a highly personalized reading guidance service to adults. After a comprehensive, in-depth discussion of an individual's needs, specific titles are suggested and book lists prepared. The service is primarily for recreational reading, and guidance is not given for school or college assignments, or to professional researchers.

Recordings

Large collections of recorded musical, non-musical, and instructional materials are available for listening or loan in the three Borough Library Centers: Donnell, Fordham (no listening facilities), and St. George, as well as the General Library & Museum of the Performing Arts at Lincoln Center. Less extensive collections of recordings can be found in a number of branches, including Mid-Manhattan Library. (Mid-Manhattan's collection includes only language materials and some spoken word recordings.)

The main repository of sound in The Research Libraries is the Rodgers and Hammerstein Archives of Recorded Sound at the Performing Arts Research Center. Other recordings collections are located at the Schomburg Center for Research in Black Culture and at the Oral Tape Archive of the Dance Collection. The latter consists of taped lectures, classes, radio interviews, together with a genuine attempt to preserve an oral history of the dance through interviews with outstanding dance personalities.

Reference Division. (See **The Research Libraries**)

The Research Libraries

The four Research Libraries of The New York Public Library together constitute one of the world's greatest reference sources—scholars' havens where every conceivable subject is pursued to its smallest detail. Among them, these facilities house over 5 million volumes, with materials in more than 3,000 languages and dialects. They are the Performing Arts Research Center; the Schomburg Center for Research in Black Culture; the Annex; and, last but hardly least, the Central Building, which has the most numerous and diverse collections of all and is headquarters of The Research Libraries as well.

Although The Research Libraries are open to the general public, with certain exceptions (see Special Collections), their facilities are mainly used by scholars, advanced students, and specialists. For the most part, people doing research below the graduate school level will find the reference materials of The Branch Libraries more than adequate, especially the extensive collections of the Mid-Manhattan Library and those of the General Library & Museum of the Performing Arts. Unlike the materials of The Branch Libraries, those of The Research Libraries do not circulate, but are restricted to use within the Library building.

Reserving Books

You may reserve books in nearly every branch library by purchasing reserve postal cards for a small charge. The card will be mailed to you when your book becomes available. Donnell Library Center reserves nonfiction only. Mid-Manhattan Library also reserves nonfiction only except for the Popular Library which does not accept any reserves. Reserves are not accepted on children's books or recordings.

The various divisions of The Research Libraries have reserve shelves, as well. Out-of-towners intending to visit New York City and wishing to use materials in The Research Libraries may, by notifying the Library in advance, reserve at no cost any title listed in the Book Catalog.

Rodgers and Hammerstein Archives of Recorded Sound
Performing Arts Research Center at Lincoln Center

The Archives are The Research Libraries' repositories of recorded sound, comprising nearly 200,000 recordings, mostly discs but including reproducible sound in all its media, old and new. In order that no future collector's item slips by, the collection of contemporary long-playing records is as comprehensive as it can be made. Among the Archives' unique items are a number of Mapleson cylinders, a remarkable amateur attempt to capture portions of actual performances given at the Metropolitan Opera in 1901-03. The holdings also include jazz and popular music, poetry and drama, the voices of famous personalities, from politicians and statesmen to entertainers and sportsmen.

S

St. George Library Center
10 Hyatt Street, Staten Island

This is Staten Island's largest library. In addition to an extensive general collection, it has sizeable holdings in education and large print books, a fine record library with listening facilities, and a spacious, well-equipped children's room. The reference collection is especially strong in the areas of business, Staten Island history, civil service materials, vocational materials, and college catalogs. There are also complete microfilm files of **The New York Times** and **Staten Island Advance** from 1921 to date.
Of special interest is the Library for the Blind Center for Staten Island which is located here. It offers Staten Island residents who are registered with it most of the same services and materials as those provided by the Library for the Blind and Physically Handicapped.

Sales Shops

The Library has two Sales Shops: one just inside the Central Building's Fifth Avenue entrance, the other on the plaza level of the Library & Museum of the Performing Arts. Both sell books, posters, games, Library souvenirs, and cards that are reproductions of Library treasures. Dandy places to pick up an unusual gift.

Schomburg Center for Research in Black Culture
103 West 135th Street

This Research Libraries facility is devoted exclusively to black life and history, and is considered one of the world's most important centers for black studies. International in scope, it covers every phase of black activity, wherever blacks have lived in significant numbers. Its materials range from early rarities to current happenings, from Mississippi to Mali.

The Center provides books of black authorship and literary and historical works in which accounts of black life and history appear. Of special interest are the histories of ancient African kingdoms and the large holdings of West Indian and Haitian materials. Also there are numerous magazines, pamphlets, pictures, photographs, newspaper clippings, broadsides, playbills, programs, and several thousand recordings of music composed or performed by blacks, which may be listened to in the library. On display at the Center is the Eric de Kolb Collection of African Arms, and objects in ivory, metal and wood.

Science Department—Mid-Manhattan Library
4th Floor, 8 East 40th Street

This Department covers the physical and life sciences, pure and applied. The collection includes hundreds of periodicals, in original form and on microfilm, and numerous indexing and abstracting services. Reference books include general and special encyclopedias, handbooks, and dictionaries as well as specialized bibliographies and biographies of scientists. There are strong collections in mathematics, physics, astronomy, the life sciences, and engineering technologies. In addition, there are scientific and technical books suitable for the non-specialist, and books covering cookery, crafts, health and nutrition, photography, and how-to-do-it materials. Most of the Department's titles are represented by both reference and circulating copies.

Science and Technology Research Center
Room 121, Central Building

The Center is one of the world's great research collections in the pure and applied physical sciences, and in related technologies and industrial arts. As such, it naturally has its share of rarities and treasures, among them early editions of Euclid's **Elementa Geometriae** and Galileo's **Dialogo.** But more important to the scientist and scholar are the long runs of technical periodicals, files of government documents, and proceedings of congresses and conferences; the Center collects and catalogs them all, numbering into the thousands. In addition, hundreds of thousands of books, from all countries and in all languages, comprehensively cover every subject area. Life sciences, however, are collected only in a limited way, and though The Research Libraries do not collect in any depth in medicine, dentistry, or pharmacy, indexing and abstracting tools are made available in these fields. **New Technical Books,** published ten times a year by The Research Libraries, is a selective, annotated list of noteworthy English-language books compiled from the many new titles submitted for the monthly exhibits of new technical books in the Center.

Slavonic Division
Room 217, Central Building

This Division covers Slavic and Baltic languages. It collects materials in Russian, Byelorussian, Ukrainian, Bulgarian, Old Church Slavonic, Serbo Croatian, Polish, Czech, Slovak, Slovenian, Lusatian, and in Moldavian (Rumanian in Cyrillic script), Latvian and Lithuanian, although these latter three are not Slavonic languages. The Division houses books, magazines, and newspapers published in any of these languages as well as all materials, regardless of language, relating to Balto-Slavic languages and literature. A great pride of the Division is its unique collection of books printed in Russia under Peter the Great—the first books printed in modern Russia. **The Dictionary Catalog of the Slavonic Division** has been published in book form. It will be supplemented.

Special Collections
Central Building

Certain very rare and unusual materials held by The Research Libraries are grouped together according to subject in what are known as the Special Collections. There are six of these: the Arents Collections, the Berg Collection, the Manuscripts and Archives Division, the Prints Division, the Rare Book Division, and the Spencer Collection. Admission to the Collections is restricted to those who can prove that their research requires them to work with these materials and to students engaged in degree programs of graduate study.

Application to use the Collections should be made through the Administrative Office, Room 214.

Special Study Areas
Central Building

Space has been set aside in the Central Building for people who are engaged in certain special kinds of activity. Permission to use these facilities should be made through the Administrative Office in Room 214.

Typing Room: Located in Room 310, it is provided for readers using library materials. Unfortunately, due to space limitations, the room is restricted to use by students on the graduate level and to those engaged in independent research. Users must supply their own typewriters, which will be checked in and out of the building by guards. Two machines are available for rent at the Delivery Desk in the Main Reading Room for those who are copying from Library materials. Locker space may be available. Typewriters may not be used in any of the reading rooms.

Wertheim Study: Room 315S, exclusively for scholars on research projects requiring extensive use of research materials. As the study is part of the Main Reading Room, typewriters, dictaphones, tape recorders and the like may not be used. Initial assignments are for three months; renewals are granted.

Frederick Lewis Allen Room: Room 112 is a study equipped with individual desks, shelf space, and lockers. It is for professional authors who are preparing books under contract. Typewriters may be used here.

Spencer Collection
Room 324, Central Building

The Collection was created by the bequest of William Augustus Spencer of his own collection of books, and an endowment fund to form a collection "representative of the arts of illustration and bookbinding," of any country and in any language. It now ranges from illuminated manuscripts on through the history of printed books, from incunabula through the successive periods of woodcut, engraving, etching, and lithography to books illustrated in any of these media by contemporary artists. (It does not include books illustrated with reproductions, except for a few accompanied by some of the original drawings.) Beyond those in the Roman alphabet, the arts of illustration and binding are represented in manuscripts or printed books from around the world, as can be seen from the following partial list: Arabic, Armenian, Chinese, Cyrillic, Ethiopic, Hebrew, Greek, Indian, Japanese, Persian, Thai, and Turkish.

The Collection's Dictionary Catalog was published in two volumes in 1971. It will be supplemented.

A card of admission must be obtained from the Administrative Office, Room 214.

Subject Directories
Central Building

Directories of subjects covered in The Research Libraries are located inside the Fifth Avenue entrance, to the left of the Inquiry Desk, and inside the Forty-second Street entrance. The directories alphabetically list the subjects and give the numbers for the Central Building rooms in which they can be found (or other locations, if not in the Central Building).

t

Telephone Reference Service
Telephone 790-6161

The Service provides answers to a wide variety of questions.
But if specialized or involved information cannot be given,
the call is transferred to a department of the Mid-Manhattan
Library, the Donnell Library Center, or to the appropriate
Research Libraries. Requests involving assignments and
contest questions won't be handled. Telephone Reference
Service also serves as a centralized source of information
about the Library, its services and activities.

Theatre Collection
Performing Arts Research Center at Lincoln Center

"Theatre" is perhaps too narrow a term for this incredible
Collection, which ranges over every phase of theatrical art
and the entertainment world, including drama, stage,
cinema, radio, television, circus, fairs, vaudeville, magic,
and minstrels. Vast files of clippings from newspapers and
magazines, under some 15,000 headings, help to speed
research and pinpoint information quickly. Photographs,
prints, posters, motion picture and television stills run into
the hundreds of thousands, programs and playbills over a
million.
The American stage and screen are admirably covered
(1870-1920) in the Robinson Locke Collection of Dramatic
Scrapbooks. The superb Hiram Stead Collection covers the
British theater between 1672 and 1932. The Parisian stage
of the eighteenth and nineteenth centuries is the subject of
the Henin Collection, which includes many original
drawings for costumes and scenery. And here, too, is one of
the largest book and periodical collections of any public
institution dealing with motion pictures. There are also
manuscripts, drafts, and typescripts of Edward Albee,
Samuel Taylor, and Edward Goodman, among others.
Printed copies of plays are not included here, however. They
can be found in the General Library & Museum of the
Performing Arts.

Typewriters and Tape Recorders

Typewriters may **not** be used in the Central Building except in the Typing Room and the Frederick Lewis Allen Room. (See also Special Study Areas). Two machines are available for rent in the Main Reading Room for those who are copying from Library materials. Arrangements should be made at the Delivery Desk.
Typewriters are permitted in the following locations at the Performing Arts Research Center: **Dance Collection**—a special area has been set aside for typewriters in the Reading Room. **Music Division**—in the Scholar's Room, which is part of the Special Collections Reading Room. **Theatre Collection**—in the Reserve Reading Room.
The Schomburg Center allows use of manual typewriters on the second floor only.
Typewriters may not be used in branch libraries.
People who supply their own tape recorders may use them in The Research Libraries to transcribe Library materials. In the Central Building make arrangements at the Delivery Desk of the Main Reading Room. At the Performing Arts Research Center arrangements should be made with the head of the division or collection concerned.
The Schomburg Center provides recording facilities for those who do not have their own machine. Consult the librarian there.
Tape recorders are usually not permitted in branch libraries.

Universal Return

Material borrowed from one branch of the Library may be returned to any other, with the exception of films, records, and pictures. These must be returned to the branch they came from.

Videotapes

The Dance Collection and the Theatre Collection of the Performing Arts Research Center collect videotapes of live performances and interviews with artists, and these are available to qualified researchers. Electronic Video Recording machines are available for viewing at the following branches: Hamilton Fish, Inwood, 125th Street, Donnell (Nathan Straus Young Adult Library), and St. George. One hundred tapes, selected from the National Audiovisual Center collection in Washington, D.C. are provided to branches under a participating program.

Vocational Information

Many branches have books and pamphlets on occupations in general and specific vocations, particularly for student use. Large reference collections of pamphlets in these areas will be found at the Fordham Library Center and the St. George Library Center.
The History and Social Science Department of the Mid-Manhattan Library has an extensive collection of books for reference and circulation, supplemented by a reference pamphlet collection. This material is suitable for the student, guidance counselor, and general reader. (See Civil Service)

Young Adult Services

Although young adults are encouraged to make full use of adult collections and services, the Library gives a great deal of attention to the special needs and requirements of teenagers. It has, in fact, provided them with a library of their very own. The Nathan Straus Young Adult Library, at Donnell Library Center, is one of the few of its kind in the country. Devoted to serving youngsters from eighth grade through high school and teachers and adults interested in teenagers, its collection of books and magazines reflects the current depth and range of teenage interests. Exhibits and programs presented through various media provide a continuing showcase for the creative activity of New York City teenagers. The Young Adult Library offers a circulating collection of books with heavy duplication of titles in paperbacks. It also features a reference collection and a considerable selection of college catalogs and vocational materials. Reading assistance and suggestions are available to teenagers, parents, authors, publishers, and librarians who work with teenagers. Visits to the Library may be made by appointment for public, private, and parochial school classes, and for community organizations.
In addition to the Young Adult Library, books of special interest to teenagers have been set aside in almost every branch. Films, concerts, book discussions, poetry workshops, videotape workshops, and other programs for young people are scheduled at Donnell and elsewhere. The Office of Young Adult Services coordinates all of the Library's teenage programs and activities. It also compiles and edits publications such as the Library's annual **Books for the Teen Age.**

Subject Directory

This directory gives the locations of the Library's most extensive collections in each subject. Numerals in the right hand column are Central Building Room numbers. Letter/numeral symbols indicate departments of Mid-Manhattan Library as follows: Cc, Popular Library; Cc1, Literature & Language; Cc2, General Reference; Cc3, Science; Cc4, History & Social Science. Page numbers refer to entries in the Guide which describe the subject's library location.

Directory of Libraries of
The New York Public Library

Research Libraries

Central Building	Fifth Ave & 42 St	790-6252
Annex	521 West 43 St	790-6354
Performing Arts Research Center at Lincoln Center	111 Amsterdam Ave	799-2200
Schomburg Center for Research in Black Culture	103 West 135 St	862-4000

Manhattan Branch Libraries

Aguilar	174 East 110 St	534-2930
Bloomingdale	150 West 100 St	222-8030
Cathedral	564 Lexington Ave	753-3066
Chatham Square	33 East Broadway	964-6598
Columbia	535 West 114 St	864-2530
Columbus	742 Tenth Ave	586-5098
Countee Cullen	104 West 136 St	281-0700
Donnell	20 West 53 St	790-6463
Epiphany	228 East 23 St	683-9845
58th Street	127 East 58 St	759-7358
Fort Washington	535 West 179 St	927-3533
General Library & Museum of the Performing Arts at Lincoln Center	111 Amsterdam Ave	799-2200
George Bruce	518 West 125 St	662-9727
Hamilton Fish Park	415 East Houston St	673-2290
Hamilton Grange	503 West 145 St	926-2147
Harlem	9 West 124 St	348-5620
Hudson Park	10 Seventh Ave South	243-6876
Inwood	4790 Broadway	942-2445
Jefferson Market	425 Ave of the Americas	243-4334
Kips Bay	446 Third Ave	683-2520
Library for the Blind and Physically Handicapped	166 Ave of the Americas	925-1011
Macomb's Bridge	2650 Seventh Ave	281-4900
Mid-Manhattan	8 East 40 St	790-6574
Muhlenberg	209 West 23 St	924-1585
96th Street	112 East 96 St	289-0908
115th Street	203 West 115 St	666-9393
125th Street	224 East 125 St	534-5050
Ottendorfer	135 Second Ave	674-0947
Picture Collection	Fifth Ave & 42 St	790-6101
Riverside	190 Amsterdam Ave	877-9186
St. Agnes	444 Amsterdam Ave	877-4380
Seward Park	192 East Broadway	477-6770
67th Street	328 East 67th St	734-1717
Tompkins Square	331 East Tenth St	228-4747
Washington Heights	1000 St. Nicholas Ave	923-6054
Webster	1465 York Ave	288-5049
Yorkville	222 East 79 St	744-5824

Bronx Branch Libraries

Allerton	2740 Barnes Ave	881-4240
Baychester	2049 Asch Loop North	379-6700
Castle Hill	2220	
	Cincinnatus Ave	824-3838
City Island	320 City Island Ave	885-1703
Clason's Point	Harrod Place	842-1235
Eastchester	1281 Burke Ave	653-3292
Edenwald	1255 East 233 St	798-3355
Fordham and		
Bronx Reference	2556 Bainbridge Ave	933-5200
Francis Martin	2150 University Ave	295-5287
Grand Concourse	155 East 173 St	872-3444
High Bridge	78 West 168 St	537-1889
Hunt's Point	877 Southern Blvd	329-2996
Jerome Park	118 Eames Place	549-5200
Kingsbridge	280 West 231 St	546-3169
Melcourt	730 Melrose Ave	292-2387
Melrose	910 Morris Ave	588-0110
Morrisania	610 East 169 St	589-9268
Mosholu	285 East 205 St	882-8239
Mott Haven	321 East 140 St	669-4878
Parkchester	1384	
	Metropolitan Ave	829-7830
Riverdale	5540 Mosholu Ave	549-1212
Sedgwick	1553 University Ave	294-1182
Soundview	660 Soundview Ave	589-0880
Spuyten Duyvil	650 West 235 St	796-1202
Throg's Neck	3817 East	
	Tremont Ave	792-2612
Tremont	1866	
	Washington Ave	299-5177
Van Cortlandt	3874 Sedgwick Ave	543-5150
Van Nest-Pelham	2147 Barnes Ave	829-5864
Wakefield	4100 Lowerre Place	652-4663
West Farms	2085 Honeywell Ave	367-5376
Westchester Square	2521 Glebe Ave	863-0436
Woodlawn Heights	4355 Katonah Ave	324-0791
Woodstock	761 East 160 St	635-9068

Staten Island Branch Libraries

Dongan Hills	1576 Richmond Road	351-1444
Great Kills	56 Giffords Lane	984-6670
Huguenot Park	904 Huguenot Ave	984-4636
New Dorp	309 New Dorp Lane	351-2977
Port Richmond	75 Bennett St	442-0158
Prince's Bay	6054 Amboy Road	356-1130
St. George	10 Hyatt St	442-8560
South Beach	100 Sand Lane	442-7420
Stapleton	132 Canal St	727-0427
Todt Hill-Westerleigh	1891 Victory Blvd	442-8373
Tottenville	7430 Amboy Road	984-0945
West New Brighton	976 Castleton Ave	442-1416

The New York Public Library is a nonprofit, tax-exempt
corporation chartered for free public service. The Library
is sustained by a combination of public and private
funds. Private contributions are needed to help provide
the services you want. Please become a FRIEND . . .
ask any librarian or guard for a FRIENDS brochure.

A GUIDE TO THE LIBRARIES OF

The New York Public Library